THE AVENUE BEARING
THE INITIAL OF CHRIST
INTO THE NEW WORLD

Books by Galway Kinnell

POETRY

What a Kingdom It Was   1960

Flower Herding on Mount Monadnock   1964

Body Rags   1968

First Poems 1946–1954   1971

The Book of Nightmares   1971

The Avenue Bearing the Initial of Christ into
the New World   1974, 2002

Mortal Acts, Mortal Words   1980

Selected Poems   1982

The Past   1985

When One Has Lived a Long Time Alone   1990

Three Books   1993, 2002

Imperfect Thirst   1994

A New Selected Poems   2000, 2001

PROSE

Black Light   1966

Walking Down the Stairs: Selections from Interviews   1978

How the Alligator Missed Breakfast (for children)   1982

The Avenue Bearing the Initial of Christ into the New World

· · · · · · · · · · · · ·

POEMS 1953–1964

Galway Kinnell

A MARINER BOOK
Houghton Mifflin Company
BOSTON   NEW YORK   2002

FIRST MARINER BOOKS EDITION 2002

Copyright 1953, 1954, © 1955, 1958, 1959, 1960, 1961, 1963, 1964, 1970, 1971, 1974, 2002 by Galway Kinnell

For information about permission to reproduce selections from this book, write to Permissions, Houghton Mifflin Company, 215 Park Avenue South, New York, New York 10003.

Visit our Web site at www.houghtonmifflinbooks.com.

Library of Congress Cataloging-in-Publication Data is available.
ISBN 0-395-18628-5
ISBN 0-618-21912-9 (pbk.)

Certain of the poems in this book have previously appeared in the following books and magazines: *The Atlantic Monthly, The Beloit Poetry Journal, Chelsea, Choice, Epoch, The Hudson Review, Modern Age, The Nation, The New Orleans Poetry Journal, New Poems by American Poets, New World Writing #3, The New Yorker, Noonday, The Paris Review, Perspective, The Pocket Book of Modern Verse, Poetry, The Prairie Schooner, The Princeton University Library Chronicle,* and *Voices.*

Book design by Anne Chalmers
Typeface: Electra

Printed in the United States of America

QUM 10 9 8 7 6 5 4 3 2 1

AUTHOR'S NOTE

This Mariner edition of *The Avenue Bearing the Initial of Christ into the New World* is a rather different book from the one that appeared under this title in 1974. *What a Kingdom It Was* and *Flower Herding on Mount Monadnock* are still here, but *First Poems 1946–1954*, included in that volume, has been dropped. I'm not really sure how *First Poems* got into that volume in the first place, unless the firm assertion in the title could, over time, have persuaded me that the book consisted of actual poems, rather than of first, frequently floundering efforts.

I have also left out poems that finally seemed unsalvageable — three from *What a Kingdom It Was* and two from *Flower Herding*. And, not surprisingly, I have taken the opportunity of this new edition to make revisions. Most of the revisions represent small interventions, but in some poems I revised rather substantially, removing material, restructuring passages, occasionally doing a little rewriting, which even to me is verboten, for I know the danger. We create by inspiration, but we revise by reason, and clarifying a murky passage may end up taking all the poetry out of it. Sometimes I've gone through a manuscript for the sole purpose of unrevising overly rational revisions.

Nevertheless, for all poets, probably for all writers, revision is an essential part of the process of composition, its last, slowed-down phase. With me, sometimes a poem comes out intact, needing the next day only a few final strokes. More commonly my first drafts grow into poems (if I am lucky) that are far longer and more complicated than those first scribblings on the back of an envelope. I don't recommend or approve of protracted alterations, but I have to accept that for me the process of revision can go on for an absurd length of time—for as long as fifty years, in the case of a few particularly intractable poems in this book.

Galway Kinnell
Sheffield, Vermont
January 1, 2002

CONTENTS

FLOWER HERDING
ON MOUNT MONADNOCK

Part II

What a Kingdom It Was

To Charles and Diana Bell

PART I

First Song

Then it was dusk in Illinois, the small boy
After an afternoon of carting dung
Hung on the rail fence, a sapped thing
Weary to crying. Dark was growing tall
And he began to hear the pond frogs all
Calling on his ear with what seemed their joy.

Soon their sound was pleasant for a boy
Listening in the smoky dusk and the nightfall
Of Illinois, and from the fields two small
Boys came bearing cornstalk violins
And they rubbed the cornstalk bows with resins
And the three sat there scraping of their joy.

It was now fine music the frogs and the boys
Did in the towering Illinois twilight make
And into dark in spite of a shoulder's ache
A boy's hunched body loved out of a stalk
The first song of his happiness, and the song woke
His heart to the darkness and into the sadness of joy.

First Communion

The church is way over in the next county,
The same trip that last year we trekked
Carrying a sackful of ears to collect
The nickel-an-ear porcupine bounty.
Pictured on the wall over Jerusalem
Jesus is shining—in the dark he is a lamp.
On the tray he is a pastry wafer.
On the way home, there is regular talk
Of the fine preaching, before the regular jokes
Are allowed. The last time over
The same trail we brought two dollars homeward.
Now we carry the afterthought of the Lord.
Soon a funny story about Uncle Abraham:
How, being liquored up, he got locked out
By his woman; how she must have gone looking for him,
For Sam says he found them, in the morning,
Asleep in each other's arms in the haybarn.

The sunlight streams through the afternoon
Another parable over the sloughs
And yellowing grass of the prairies.
Cold wind stirs, and the last green
Climbs to all the tips of the season, like
The last flame brightening on a wick.
Embers drop and break in sparks. Across the earth
Sleep is the overlapping of enough shadows.
In the wind outside a twig snaps
Like a lid clicking shut somewhere in the ear.

Jesus, a boy thinks as his room goes out,
Jesus, it is a disappointed shed
Where they hang your picture
And drink juice, and conjure
Your person into inferior bread—
I would speak of injustice,
I would not go again into that place.

To Christ Our Lord

The legs of the elk punctured the snow's crust
And wolves floated lightfooted on the land
Hunting Christmas elk living and frozen.
Inside, snow melted in a basin, and a woman basted
A bird held by feet and wings over a coal bed.

Snow had sealed the windows, candles lit
The Christmas meal. The Christmas grace chilled
The cooked bird, being long-winded and the room cold.
During the words a boy thought, is it fitting
To eat this creature killed on the wing?

He had killed it himself, climbing out
Alone on snowshoes in the Christmas dawn,
The fallen snow swirling and the snowfall gone,
Heard its throat scream when the shotgun shouted,
Watched it drop, and fished from the snow the dead.

He had not wanted to shoot. The sound
Of wings beating into the hushed air
Had stirred his love, and his fingers
Froze in his gloves, and he wondered,
Famishing, could he fire? Then he fired.

Now the grace praised his wicked act. At its end
The bird on the plate
Stared at his stricken appetite.
There had been nothing to do but surrender,
To kill and to eat; he ate as he had killed, with wonder.

At night on snowshoes on the drifting field
He wondered again, for whom had love stirred?
The stars glittered on the snow and nothing answered.
The Swan spread her wings, cross of the cold north,
The pattern and mirror of the acts of earth.

The Wolves

Last night knives flashed. LeChien cried
And chewed blood in his bed.
Vanni's whittling blade
Had found flesh easier than wood.

Vanni and I left camp on foot. In a glade
We came on a brown blossom
Great and shining on a thorned stem.
"That's the sensitive briar," I said.

"It shrinks at the touch," I added.
Soon we found buffalo. Picking
A bull grazing by itself, I began
The approach: while the shaggy head

Was turned I sprinted across the sod,
And when he swung around his gaze
I bellyflopped into the grass
And lay on my heartbeat and waited.

When he looked away again I made
Enough yardage before he wheeled
His head: I kneeled, leveled
My rifle, and we calmly waited.

It occurred to me as we waited
That in those last moments he was,
In fact, daydreaming about something else.
"He is too stupid to live," I said.

His legs shifted and the heart showed.
I fired. He looked, trotted off,
He simply looked and trotted off,
Stumbled, sat himself down, and became dead.

I looked for Vanni. Among the cows he stood,
Only his arms moving as he fired,
Loaded, fired, the dumb herd
Milling about him sniffing at their dead.

I called and he retreated.
We cut two choice tongues for ourselves
And left the surplus. All day wolves
Would splash blood from those great sides.

Again we saw the flower, brown-red
On a thorn-spiked stem. When Vanni
Reached out his fingers, it was funny,
It shrank away as if it had just died.

They told us in camp that LeChien was dead.
None of us cared. Nobody much
Had liked him. His tobacco pouch,
I noticed, was already missing from beside his bed.

Westport

From the hilltop we could look back
At the forest, that half a continent away
Had met our fathers on the Atlantic shore.
Before us lay a narrow belt of brush.
Everywhere beyond, shifting like an ocean,
Swell upon swell of emerald green,
The prairies of the west were blowing.

We mounted and set out, small craft
Into the green. The grasses brushed
The bellies of the horses, and under
The hooves the knotted centuries of sod
Slowed the way. Here and there the grey
Backs of wolves breached and fell, as in the grass
Their awkward voyages appeared and vanished.

Then rain lashed down, a savage squall.
All afternoon it blew straight at us. "It will be
A long, hard journey," the boy said, "and look,
We are blown like the weed." *O wild indigo,*
O love-lies-bleeding, prince's feather,
Pigweed, and bugseed: you who have known
The sad ambages compassed for ourselves.

When the storm abated, a red streak in the west
Lit up the raindrops on the land before us.
"Yes," I said, "it will be a hard journey…"
The shining grasses were bowed to the ground
As if the hard rain had killed them. "But at last,"
I added, "the hardness is the thing you thank."
So out of forest we sailed onto plains,

And from the dark afternoon came a bright evening.
Now out of evening we discovered night
And heard the cries of the prairie and the moan
Of wind through the roots of its clinging flowers.

PART II

At the Reading of a Poet's Will

Item. A desk
Smelling of ink and turpentine
To anyone whose task
Is to sweat rain for a line.

Item. A sheaf
Of poems, a few lucid,
One or two brief,
To anyone who'll bid.

Item. Praise Jesus, who spent
His last cent
In the wilderness of himself in the try
For self-mastery.

Item. I built a desk,
I spent myself for a sheaf,
All else I committed I ask
That the Lord forgive.

I took Christ for my pattern,
Once he was kind to a slattern,
If I was led into mazes
Blame and praise Jesus. *Amen.*

Lilacs

The wind climbed with a laggard pace
Up the green hill. Meeting the sun there
It disappeared like hot wax
Into the ground. Down on the south slope
A dog stretched, and swaths of lilacs
Opened huge furnaces of scent.

A woman betook herself into the park,
Her dry legs crackling in darkness,
Past lilac, dog, the fierce and asleep.
Summer slopped at her knees.
She walked in the scent of herself breaking
Out of closets in the well-governed flesh.

She stopped. Blossoms climbed
And blazed in the air, the lawn slowly
Somersaulted under her. She turned back
To the narrow parlor, where tea and dry supper
Would be laid, and a spoon would arrange
The leaves on the bottom of her china dream.

A Toast to Tu Fu

To you, Tu Fu,
Because it didn't work out
When you lent
Yourself to government.
A poet may not be constituted to fix
Things up—only to celebrate
What's down, and in politics
As that Irishman found out
Is a lout.

To you, Tu Fu,
For fooling the crew
Who thought so much trial
Would make a man good;
And for, when the waters rose
Up around the temple
You clung to in the flood,
While they prayed you'd
Let go with a prayer,
Hanging on like a bear.

And again to you, Tu Fu,
For gorging at the feast
Honoring your rescue,
For not mentioning virtue
In your short speech, nor praising rot,
And for having had the appetite and timing
To die of overeating on the spot.

Easter

To get to church you have to cross the river,
First breadwinner for the town, its wide
Mud-colored currents cleansing forever
The swill-making villages at its side.

The disinfected voice of the minister
For a moment is one of the clues,
But he is talking of nothing but Easter,
Dying so on the wood, He rose.

Some of us daydream of the morning news,
Some of us lament we rose at all,
A child beside me comforts her doll,
We are dying on the hard wood of the pews.

Death is everywhere, in the extensive
Sermon, the outcry of the inaudible
Prayer, the nickels, the dimes the poor give,
And outside, at last, in the gusts of April.

Upon the river, its Walden calm,
With wire hooks the little boats are fishing.
Those who can wait to get home
Line up, and lean on the railing, wishing.

Up through the mud can you see us
Waiting here for you, for hours,
Disappeared one, trapped or working loose,
Our hats like a row of flowers?

Then we crown you with an Easter fire,
And if you do not rise before dinner
When the flower show must retire,
Then drink if you must of the breadwinner.

Tomorrow when the brown water
Shall shove you senselessly on
Past smoking cities, works of disaster,
Kids playing ball, cows, unrealistic fishermen,

Toll bridges you slip under for free,
And you look back from the brown lorry
That floats your drenched flesh to sea,
May you, moved by goodbyes, be not altogether sorry

That the dream has ended. Turn
On all that happened an unwavering gaze.
It is as you thought. The living burn.
In the floating days may you discover grace.

For William Carlos Williams

When you came and you talked and you read with your
Private zest from the varicose marble
Of the podium, the lovers of literature
Paid you the tribute of their almost total
Inattention, although someone when you spoke of a pig
Did squirm, and it is only fair to report another gig-

gled. But you didn't even care. You seemed
Above remarking we were not your friends.
You hung around inside the rimmed
Circles of your heavy glasses and smiled and
So passed a lonely evening. In an hour
Of talking, your honesty built you a tower.

When it was over and you sat down and the chair-
man got up and smiled and congratulated
You and shook your hand, I watched a professor
In neat bow tie and enormous tweeds, who patted
A faint praise of the sufficiently damned,
Drained spittle from his pipe, then scrammed.

For the Lost Generation

Oddities composed the sum of the news.
$E=mc^2$
Was another weird
Sign of the existence of the Jews.

And Paris! All afternoon in someone's attic
We lifted our glasses
And drank to the asses
Who ran the world and were all neurotic.

Ours was a wonderful party,
Everyone threw rice,
The fattest lover was nice,
The world was aswirl in wisecracks and confetti.

The War was like a first marriage, a mutual blunder.
Who was right, who lost,
Held nobody's interest,
The dog on top was as bad as the dog under.

Sometimes after whiskey, at the break of day,
There was a trace
Of puzzlement on a face,
Face of blue nights that kept bleaching away.

Look back on it all—the faraway cost,
Crash and sweet blues
(O Hiroshima, O Jews)—
No generation was so gay as the lost.

Leaping Falls

And so it was I sheered,
Eccentric, into outer space,
And tracked with lost paces
The forgotten journey of a child,
Across the creaking snow,
Up the deer-trail,

Over the snowdrifted hill
Into the secret country
Where a boy once found,
Routing from ledge to ledge
In a tumult at sunrise,
The cascading of Leaping Falls.

Now the falls lay draped
Without motion or sound,
Icicles fastened in stories
To stillness and rock. At the bottom,
A heap of broken icicles
Lay dead blue on the snow.

Cold was through and through,
Noiseless. Nothing
But clouds at my nostrils
Moved. Then I uttered a word,
Simply a bleak word
Slid from my lips. Whereupon

A topmost icicle came loose
And fell, and struck another
With a bell-like sound, and
Another, and the falls
Leapt at their ledges, ringing
Down the rocks and on each other

Like an outbreak of bells
That rings and ceases.
The silence turned around
And became silence again.
Under the falls on the snow
A twigfire of icicles burned pale blue.

Promontory Moon

The moon: she shakes off her cloaks,
Her rings of mist and circle of blurred light,
And shines without chemistry or heat
Upon us. Milky blue in her influence
The sea dabbles at the tiers of rock.
Shadowy rabbits move feinting
Over the grass and paths. Tomorrow under the sun
Men and women will sprawl generating here;
But tonight rabbits ask nothing of the moon
And run in moonlight for delight alone.

Half rabbits, half rabbits' shadows,
They are like the night-roistering fairies
For whom as children we laid banquets
In the dusk, bits of bread and honey
That, exploring for in the dawn, we found
Untouched, the one trace of them being
The dew glistening on the moss
And grass, shed perhaps for sorrow that
Their luminous bodies have no appetite,
Being woven by the night of moonlight.

The sun makes the grass increase, feeding
The things it can corrupt. The moon
Holds her purer watches on the night,
Mirroring on this fairest time of day
Only the miracles of light;
And all within ourselves too straight to bend

In agonies of death and birth—as now
The blue-white water swirls at the moonbeams
And keeps on winding on the shining clew—
Dissolves at her touch and is made anew.

Gothic Slide

Above the blue wash of the lake
Where the sun is a bright spectre,
And cars run, we discourse on culture;
Until the curtains close our modern talk
And faces in the slides revive
World-famous beauty, blent of light and grief.
Who can look on these stone figures,
The fatal innocence in these stone smiles,
And not sit there smitten, a credulous pupil?
Over the cloaked bodies and covered necks
The lips come alive, but they move alone;
How could we reply with tongues of stone?
The curtains open and our dazed eyes wreck
On the sunlight climbing like a dream
Into the darkness that had become our home.
Below, the waves return like breaths
On the shores of Chicago; sunlight weaves
In flashes over the curve of the Drive
Where the cars and cares of the earth crawl in a line.

Earth-Sparrow

The trees in clouds of November mist
Standing empty and the massive earth bare
I bent my head and leaned myself against
Interior gales and blizzards of unrest
Facing the squalor of November air

But stopped at last and skyward with shredded
Arms lifting ribbons of fingers and prayers
I caught in that beseeching of the cloud
A leafless lightning-splintered oak unshroud-
ing its wreckage in the waste of the year

To whose ultimate twig with a glide and
Dip a sparrow summitted and there burst-
ing as if the dead sap kept singing I leaned
Forward knowing nothing to lean on
Green as the grasslessness Lord of the earth.

Rain over a Continent

Rain over a continent, the train
From Washington to Washington plunged
In the sowing rain. He slept with
His nurse on the voyage, she was
Marked with transcontinental love,
She was his all-guessing heart when he died.
Raise the blind, he asked. Under
The rain the continent wheeled, his own land
Electric and blind, farmlights and cities'
Blazes—points, clusters, and chains—
Each light a memory, all of the darkness memory.

Reply to the Provinces

He writes from the provinces: it is
Shuttered and desolate there, will I please
Sit on a bench for him every so often
In the Luxembourg Gardens? So now
In the elegant autumn, to regard and guess—:

The sea-eyed children watching their sloops
Angling on the pond? Expectant in their books
The delicate young women? The would-be
Casters-off of expectation? The hands-in-hands?
The fellow shucking chestnuts for his girl?
The Algerians, Americans, English, Danes
Giving the Gardens their Parisian character?
Fountained light streaming on the wind?
Surely these and things of this kind—
Whatever is human. Also I marvel at the leaves
Yellow on the sky, and there on the grass
Where the leaves overlap, yellow, the yellow sun
Forcing a hidden glowing from the earth. So I sit
Peering like an ape on a branch, on a bench.

In the provinces he may have walked from town.
In a city of leaves he may have found her. Perhaps
Already they are lying in the leaves, amusing
Each other by pointing out all the faces in the leaves.

Near Barbizon

At first I thought some animal, wounded,
Thrashed in the brush, for the hunting horns
Had sounded last night and this morning.
No, it was only the woodgatherer
Out after lunch breaking twigs for his fire.
Others might have laid the stick across two rocks
And stomped in the middle. He raised it like a flail
And beat a boulder until the weapon broke.
We talked. It was election time, I asked
Who was he voting for. He screwed his eyes.
"If there came into your house by night
Thieves, to which would you offer your wife?"
Whacks he laid on the rock until the branch gave.
"I am too honest, *merde*, too poor to vote.
There's fuel on the forest floor still."
"What's your trade?" I inquired. "Gardener."
"So you make things bloom?" "Yes, and the pay's
Nothing." He flailed the rocks in savage, measured
Strokes. "The pay's nothing," he repeated,
Looking up without ceasing his labor, eyes
Flashing, this ignorant American, this fascist tool.

Duck-Chasing

I spied a very small brown duck
Riding the swells. "Little duck!"
I cried. It paddled away,
I paddled after it. When it dived,
Down I dived too: too smoky was the sea,
We were lost. It surfaced
In the west, I swam west
And when it dived I dived,
And we were lost and lost and lost
In the slant smoke of the sea.
When I came floating up on it
From the side, like a deadman,
And yelled suddenly, it took off,
It skimmed the swells as it ascended,
Brown wings burning and flashing
In the sun as the sea it rose over
Burned and flashed underneath it.
I did not see the little duck again.
Duck-chasing is a game like any game.
When it is over it is all over.

For Ruth

It was a surprise,
Seeing you. You were
More steadfast than I remember.
On the limestone shelf
You endured yourself
With grace.

The shock was only
When you laid in on tape
Some of my speech, to escape
Into or to live through
Later, when you could get blue—
But of course you would be lonely,

You of that fierce memory!
I saw you once remembering
A fisherman drunk as bait on a string
At the end of the bar—
Your chilled flesh went blue as a star.
A thing turns real eventually,

The touch is just the babytooth.
On your heap of bleached rock
You listen, wires in the mind play it back,
You hear the million sighs,
You cry for them, each cries
For ruth, for ruth.

In a Parlor Containing a Table

In a parlor containing a table
And three chairs, three men confided
Their inmost thoughts to one another.
I, said the first, am miserable.
I am miserable, the second said.
I think that for me the right word
Is miserable, said the third.
Well, they said, it's quarter to two.
Good night. Cheer up. Sleep well.
You too. You too. You too.

Guillaume de Lorris

His is the romance without a heroine —
Only the Rose in the Garden, far away,
Restless in shadows, longing to be plucked.
The intensity of his dream nourishing him
The hero walks the desert of this world
Toward, without swerving, *l'idéale Bien-Aimée.*

He comes into the Garden on broken feet
After many years: he discovers at last,
Unattended, the mysterious Rose.
Being old at this moment (he has walked
Half his life on the desert), he declines,
Out of pity, to take what he has just to take.

Suddenly, however, he remembers the quest —
The days of solitude, when everywhere,
It seemed, others were happy on the earth.
Old in his heart, now pale as the desert,
He looks for her. He sees her in the arms
Of young men, she is shedding tears for him.

Toward the Wilderness

Trekking the desert the man feels
The atmosphere weigh on him like a knapsack.
He knows the fix upon him of eyes
Hung from huge wings frayed at the edges
Floating dead and black in the sky.

And the Dead Sea, that will neither
Renew nor drown him, a glow rubbed
Into the sand, shimmers under the range
In which Nebo can be picked out
As the historic, tall, and bleak one.

He puts the bead of his will on the peak
And does not waver. His plan is
To look over the far side of the mount
On which Moses died looking this way,
And see the bitter land, and die of desire.

PART III

The Schoolhouse

1

I find it now, the schoolhouse by the tree,
And through the broken door, in brown light,
I see the benches in rows, the floor he
Paced across, the windows where the fruit
Took the shapes of hearts, and the leaves windled
In the fall, and winter snowed on his head.

In this wreck of a house we were taught
Everything we thought a man could know,
All action, all passion, all ancient thought,
What Socrates had got from Diotima,
How Troilus laughed, in tears, in paradise,
That crowns leapfrog through blood: casts of the dice.

The door hangs from one hinge. Maybe the last
Schoolboy simply forgot to lift the latch
When he rushed out that spring, in his haste —
Or maybe that same boy, now fat and rich,
Snow-haired in his turn, and plagued by thought,
Bulled his way back in, looking for the dead light.

2

A man of letters once asked the local tramps
To tea. No one came, and he read from Otway
And Chatterton to the walls, and lived for months
On the crumpets. They padlocked the gate when he died.

Snow, sleet, rain, piss of tramps, until one year
The lock snapped, the hinges rasped like roosters.

And now when the tramps, waking sheeted in frost,
Know it is time, they come here and sprawl
At the foot of the statue they think is of their host,
Which they call "His Better Self," which he had called
"Knowledge," sometimes "Death," whose one gesture
Seems to beckon and yet remains obscure,

And boil their tea on the floor and pick fruit
In the garden where he used to walk
Thinking of Eden and the fallen state,
And dust an apple as he had a book—
"Hey now Porky, gie's the core," one hollers;
"Wise up," says Pork, "they ain't gonna *be* a core."

3

I hear modern schoolchildren shine their pants
In buttock-soothing seats in steamy schools
Soaking up civics and vacant events
From innocents who sponge periodicals
And clop-clop the stuff out again in chalky gray
Across the blackboards of the modern day;

Yet they can guess why we fled our benches
Afternoons when we ourselves were just nice
Schoolkids too, who peered out through the branches
For one homely share of the centuries,
Fighting in Latin the wars of the Greeks,
Our green days, the apple we picked and picked

And that was never ours; though they would
Rake their skulls if they found out we returned
By free choice to this house of the dead,
And stand wondering what he could have learned,
His eyes great pupils and his fishhook teeth
Sunk in the apple of knowledge or death.

4

I recall a recitation in that house:
"*We are the school of Hellas* was the claim.
Maybe it was so. Anyway Hellas
Thought it wasn't, and put the school to flame.
They came back, though, and scavenged the ruins."
I think the first inkling of the lesson

Was when we watched him from the apple wrest
Something that put the notion in his brain
The earth was coming to its beautifulest
And would be like paradise again
The day he died from it. The flames went out
In their blue mantles; he waved us to the night—

And we are here, under the starlight. I
Remember he taught us the stars disperse
In wild flight, though constellated to the eye.
Now I can almost see the night in its course,
The slow sky uncoiling in exploding forms,
The stars that flee it riding free in its arms.

Seven Streams of Nevis

1

Jack the Blindman, whose violin
Through the harsh weathers of the street
Lifted a scraping bright and sweet,
Joked the gloomier bars of every tune;
But hardly a dime ever dropped there
And he cupped *faith* in the clankless air.

Connelly, one-eyed, half blind,
Finding the world blind, in full view
Like wind blew ropes and fences through.
Ticketless at the stiles of the mind
We ask his *hope:* down, and out,
To swear, "If scum swims to the top of the sauerkraut..."

They didn't sign up at the desk
Or queue at the bed, though they clapped
The night you bumped and shook and slapped
And ground for free your smart burlesque,
Peaches. We call it *mercy* when
You give and get nothing and give again.

Tossing in dreams young David Boyle
Could not evade the call of the Lord
For the meek life. He woke and poured
Over his heart the scalding oil
Of *temperance.* Now in his sleep
He yells aloud to God to let him sleep.

Justice made James Lynch Fitzstephen
Hang from a tree his guilty son;
His heart, twice guilty then,
Hanged itself in his skeleton.
Even Cicero would have known
The unjust who are just are just mad bone.

Natasha, who billowed like silk
On a pole of fire, and weeping went
To one who scrapes the burning tent
While he puffs Luckies and sips milk,
And came home like an empty cage
To find home yet emptier, tried *courage*.

Sir Henry, seeing that the dew
Gets burned each morning into mist,
Decided fire brings out the best
In things, and that anyone who
Cooks his eyes at the sunrise
Of the beautiful, and renders himself blind, is *wise*.

2

In darkness I climbed Ben Nevis, far from
Your lives. But the seven streams I came on
Were well foreknown. One sang like strings, one crashed
Through gated rocks, one vibrated, others
Went skipping like unbucketed oil across
Hot stones, or clattered like bones, or like milk
Spilled and billowed in streamers of bright silk:
Irises glimmering a visionary course,

Me grimping the dark, sniffing for the source;
And there I found it windless, lying still,
Dark, high-nested in the mountain, a pool
Whose shined waters on the blackened mountain
Held the black skies; and I rode out on the water
And the waves ringing through the dark were rings
Around the eye itself of the world, which,
Drawing down heaven like its black lid, was there
Where merely to be still was temperate,
Where to move was brave, where justice was a glide,
Knowledge the dissolving of the head-hung eyes;
And there my faith lay burning, there my hope
Was burning on the water, there charity
Burned like a sun. Oh give, O pool of heaven,
The locus of grace to seven who are whirled
Down the eddies and gutters of the world;
And Connelly and Jack and Peaches, Dave,
Lynch, Natalie, and Hank—seven who have
Bit on your hearts, and spat the gravels of
Tooth and heart, and bit again; who have wiped
The burst jellies of eyes on a sleeve
(The visions that could have been wrung from that cloth)
And sprouted sight like mushrooms—O seven
Streams of nothing backgazing after heaven,
In the heart's hell you have it, it is called God's Love.

The Descent

1

Nailed by our axes to the snow
We belayed. One by one we climbed.
Had somebody in the valley
Been looking up, it must have seemed
A crazed earthworm headed for paradise,
Or else, if he happened to rub his eyes

While we unroped, and to look back
When we had scattered in the race
For the crest, an ascension of crows.
I took the crest as the day broke,
Sure I was first. But Jan must have leapt
The crevasse for a shortcut: he lay there,

Blue lips apart, on the blue snow,
Sprawled on the shellbursts of his heart.
"It's time it went," he gasped. Four years
He had fought in the guerrilla wars.
Then he whispered, "Look—the sunrise!"
The same color and nearly the same size,

But behind his back, the sun
Was rising. When the moon he was
Staring at set in the mountains
He died. On the way back the ice
Had turned so perilous under the sun
There was no choice: we watched while he went down.

2

In Seekonk Woods, on Indian Hill,
It used to seem the branches made
A small green sky that gave off shade.
Once while I lay buried like a quail
In the grass and shadows, a shotgun
Banged, leaves burst, I blinked into the sunshine —

Two crows blown out from either hand
Went clattering away; a third
Thumped through the branches to the ground.
I scooped it up, splashed across the ford,
And lit out — I must have run half a day
Before I reached Holy Spring. (Anyway,

I thought it was holy. No one
Had told me heaven is overhead.
I only knew people look down
When they pray.) I held the dying bird
As though, should its heartbeat falter,
There wouldn't be any heartbeat anywhere.

After a while I touched the plumes
To the water. In the desert
By the tracks I dug a headstart
Taller than myself. I told him,
"Have a good journey. It can't be far.
It'll be well this side of China, for sure."

3

And had I faced Jan to the sun
Might not the sun have held him here?
Or did he know the day came on
Behind, not glancing back for fear
The full moon already was dragging from his bones
The blood as dear to them, and as alien,

As clothes to a scarecrow
Or flesh to a cross? Down snow,
Following streambeds through the trees,
We sledded him. To his valleys
Rivers have washed this adept of the sun
The moon pestled into earth again.

Heaven is in light, overhead,
I have it by heart. Yet the dead
Silting the darkness do not ask
For burials elsewhere than the dusk.
They lie where nothing but the moon can rise,
And make no claims, though they had promises.

Milkweed that grow beside the tombs
Climb from the dead as if in flight,
But a foot high they stop and bloom
In drab shapes, that neither give light
Nor bring up the true darkness of the dead;
Strange, homing lamps, that go out seed by seed.

4

I looked for Indian Hill at Easter.
It was bulldozed. A TV cross
Gleamed from the rooftop of a house
Like sticks of a scarecrow. Once more
I turned and ran: I stumbled on
Fields lying dark and savage and the sun

Reaping its own fire from the trees,
Whirling the faint panic of birds
Up turbulent light. Two white-haired
Crows cried under the wheeling rays;
And loosed as by a scythe, into the sky
A flight of jackdaws rose, earth-birds suddenly

Seized by some thaumaturgic thirst,
Shrill wings flung up the crow-clawed, burned,
Unappeasable air. And then one turned,
Dodged through the flock again, and burst
Eastward alone, sinking across the trees
On the world-curve of its wings. So it is,

Mirrored in duskfloods, the fisherbird
Stands in a desolate sky
Feeding at its own heart. In the cry
Eloi! Eloi! flesh was made word:
We hear it in wind catching in the branches.
In lost blood breaking a night through the bones.

Where the Track Vanishes

1

The snow revives in the apple trees;
The winter sun seeps from jonquils
Bright as goldmills on the slopes;
Le chemin montant dans les hautes herbes
Curves for the Alps and vanishes.

2

Pierre le Boiteux
—Yellow teeth
Gnashed into gum-level
Stumps, yellow
Eyes beaconing about,
A blackhead the size
Of a huckleberry
Making a cheek sag,
A leg gypsies
Cut the tendon of
So he could beg better as a child
Pumping under him,
Twelve goats at heel—
Mounts the track,
Limping through the wild
Grasses—toward where?

3

The track vanishes in a heap of stones
Mortared by weeds and wildflowers—
The fallen church. Nearby stand stones
Of the parish graves, dates worn away,
A handful of carved words visible:
Jacques et Geneviève, priez pour eux—
Véronique DuPrès, regrets éternels—
Sown here even to their fingertips.

Who was it wore the track through the grass?
Surely their mourners are dead, and theirs, and theirs.
Perhaps Pierre limps up every day
Training the goats where to come when it is time,
Foreseeing a terrible loneliness.
No one is lonely here: take Véronique—Jacques,
Husband of another, indifferently dissolves into her.
A skull or two, a couple of pelvises or knees.

4

My hand on the sky
Cannot shut the sky out
Any more than any March
Branch can. In the Boston Store
Once, I tried new shoes:
The shoeman put my feet
Into a machine, saying Kid
Wrig yer toes. I

Wrigged and peered:
Inside green shoes green
Twigs were wrigging by themselves
Green as the grasses
I drew from her
Hair in the springtime
While she laughed, unfoliaged
By sunlight, a little
Spray of bones I loved.

5

From villages lost in the valleys—
Moncharvet, St. Bon, La Jaura—
Thin braids of smoke waver upward
Through the clear air. A few lights
Come on, visible from the untracked snow
On the stairway to the Alps. Venus
Shines from the grave of the sun, like
The white gem churched again in its valley.

Once driving from Morristown at night,
We came over a crest: the Fish-Island
Breached shining under the strung-out stars
Of the Galaxy—a long way from Jacques
And Geneviève and Véronique in her prairie.
We stood there not thinking that for them
This would be a strange continent to be dying in,
This starry island under the continent of the stars—

Job's Coffin and the Scorpion; Jacques
And Geneviève side by side in the field of light;
Capricorn, Ophiocus; the Serpent embracing
The unhinged knees, St. Bon heaped
In its molted skin; Le Fourmier the arms
Of Hercules; the Swan sailing toward Planay;
Moncharvet, La Jaura by the singing Lyre;
Véronique rocked on the Balances; Champ Béranger—

Fields into which the Herdsman limps
Leading his flock up the trackless night, toward
A writhing of lights. Are they Notre Dame des Neiges
Where men ask their God for the daily bread—
Or the March-climbing Virgin carrying wheat?
Where the track vanishes the first land begins.
It goes out everywhere obliterating the horizons.
We may have been walking through it all our lives.

Freedom, New Hampshire

1

We came to visit the cow
Dying of fever,
Towle said it was already
Shoveled under, in a secret
Burial-place in the woods.
We prowled through the woods
Weeks, we never

Found where. Other
Children other summers
Must have found the place
And asked, Why is it
Green here? The rich
Guess a grave, maybe,
The poor think a pit

For dung, like the one
We shoveled in in the fall,
That came up a brighter green
The next year, that
Could as well have been
The grave of a cow
Or something, for all that shows.

2

We found a cowskull once; we thought it was
From one of the asses in the Bible, for the sun
Shone into the holes through which it had seen
Earth as an endless belt carrying gravel, had heard
Its truculence cursed, had learned how human sweat
Stinks, and had brayed—shone into the holes
With solemn and majestic light, as if some
Skull somewhere could be Baalbek or the Parthenon.

That night passing Towle's Barn
We saw lights. Towle had lassoed a calf
By its hind legs, and he tugged against the grip
Of the darkness. The cow stood by, chewing millet.
Derry and I took hold, too, and hauled.
It was sopping with darkness when it came free.
It was a bullcalf. The cow mopped it awhile,
And we walked around it with a lantern,

And it was sunburned, somehow, and beautiful.
It took a teat as the first business
And sneezed and drank at the milk of light.
When we got it balanced on its legs, it went wobbling
Toward the night. Walking home in darkness
We saw the July moon looking on Freedom, New Hampshire,
We smelled the fall in the air, it was the summer,
We thought, Oh this is but the summer!

3

Once I saw the moon
Drift into the sky like a bright
Pregnancy pared
From a goddess who had to
Keep slender to remain beautiful—
Cut loose, and drifting up there
To happen by itself—
And waning, in lost labor;

As we lost our labor
Too—afternoons
When we sat on the gate
By the pasture, under the Ledge,
Buzzing and skirling on toilet-
papered combs tunes
To the rumble-seated cars
Taking the Ossipee Road

On Sundays; for
Though dusk would come upon us
Where we sat, and though we had
Skirled out our hearts in the music,
Yet the not-yet dandruffed
Harps we skirled it on
Had done not much better than
Flies, which buzzed, when quick

We trapped them in our hands,
Which went silent when we
Crushed them, which we bore
Downhill to the meadowlark's
Nest full of throats, which
Derry charmed and combed
With an Arabian air, while I
Chucked crushed flies into

Innards I could not see,
For the night had fallen
And the crickets shrilled on all sides
In waves, as if the grassleaves
Shrieked by hillsides
As they grew, and the stars
Made small flashes in the sky,
Like mica flashing in rocks

On the chokecherried Ledge
Where bees I stepped on once
Hit us from behind like a shotgun,
And where we could see
Windowpanes in Freedom flash
And Loon Lake and Winnipesaukee
Flash in the sun
And the blue world flashing.

4

The fingerprints of our eyeballs would zigzag
On the sky; the clouds that came drifting up

Our fingernails would drift into the thin air;
In bed at night there was music if you listened,
Of an old surf breaking far away in the blood.

Children who come by chance on grass green for a man
Can guess cow, dung, man, anything they want,
To them it is the same. To us who knew him as he was
After the beginning and before the end, it is green
For a name called out of the confusions of the earth —

Winnipesaukee coined like a moon, a bullcalf
Dragged from the darkness where it breaks up again,
Larks which long since have crashed for good in the grass
To which we fed the flies, buzzing ourselves like flies,
While the crickets shrilled beyond us, in July.

The mind may sort it out and give it names —
When a man dies he dies trying to say without slurring
The abruptly decaying sounds. It is true
That only flesh dies, and spirit flowers without stop
For men, cows, dung, for all dead things; and it is good, yes —

But an incarnation is in particular flesh
And the dust that is swirled into a shape
And crumbles and is swirled again had but one shape
That was this man. When he is dead the grass
Heals what he suffered, but he remains dead,
And the few who loved him know this until they die.

For my brother, 1925–1957

The Supper After the Last

1

The desert moves out on half the horizon
Rimming the illusory water which, among islands,
Bears up the sky. The sea scumbles in
From its inviolate border under the sky.
A dragonfly floating on six legs on the sand
Lifts its green-yellow tail, declines its wings
A little, flutters them a little, and lays
On dazzled sand the shadow of its wings. Near shore
A bather wades through his shadow in the water.
He tramples and kicks it; it recomposes.

2

Outside the open door
Of the whitewashed house,
Framed in the doorway, a chair,
Vacant, waits in the sunshine.

A jug of fresh water stands
Inside the door. In the sunshine
The chair waits, less and less vacant.
The host's plan is to offer water, then stand aside.

3

They eat chicken, drink rosé. The chicken's head
Has been tucked under the shelter of its wing.
Under the table a red-backed, passionate dog
Cracks chicken bones on the blood and gravel floor.

No one else but the dog and the blind
Cat watching it knows who is that bearded
Wild man guzzling overhead, the wreck of passion
Emptying his eyes, who has not yet smiled,

Who stares at the company, where he is company,
Turns them to sacks of appalled, grinning skin,
Forks the fowl-eye out from under
The large, makeshift, cooked lid, evaporates the wine,

Jellies the sunlit table and spoons, floats
The deluxe grub down the intestines of the Styx,
Devours all but the cat, to whom he slips scraps, and the dog,
The red-backed accomplice busy grinding gristle.

4

When the bones of the host
Crack in the hound's jaw
The wild man rises. Opening
His palms he announces:
I came not to astonish
But to destroy you. Your

Jug of cool water? Your
Hanker after wings? Your
Lech for transcendence?
I came to prove you are
Intricate and simple things
As you are, created
In the image of nothing,
Taught of the creator
By your images in dirt —
As mine, for which you set
A chair in the sunshine,
Mocking me with water!
As pictures of wings,
Not even iridescent,
That clasp the sand
And that cannot perish, you swear,
Having once been evoked!

5

The witnesses back off; the scene begins to float in water.
Far out in that mirage the Savior sits whispering to the world,
Becoming a mirage. The dog turns into a smear on the sand.
The cat grows taller and taller as it flees into space.

From the hot shine where he sits his whispering drifts:
You struggle from flesh into wings; the change exists.
But the wings that live gripping the contours of the dirt
Are all at once nothing, flesh and light lifted away.

You are the flesh; I am the resurrection, because I am the light.
I cut to your measure the creeping piece of darkness
That haunts you wherever you go. Step into light—
I make you over. I breed the shape of your grave in the dirt.

PART IV

The Avenue Bearing the Initial of Christ into the New World

Was diese kleine Gasse doch für ein Reich an sich war...

1

pcheek pcheek pcheek pcheek pcheek
They cry. The motherbirds thieve the air
To appease them. A tug on the East River
Blasts the bass-note of its passage, lifted
From the infra-bass of the sea. A broom
Swishes over the sidewalk like feet through leaves.
Valerio's pushcart Ice Coal Kerosene
Moves   clack
               clack
                   clack
On a broken wheelrim. Ringing in its chains
The New Star Laundry horse comes down the street
Like a roofleak whucking into a pail.
At the redlight, where a horn blares,
The Golden Harvest Bakery brakes on its gears,
Squeaks, and seethes in place. A propane-
gassed bus makes its way with big, airy sighs.

Across the street a woman throws open
Her window.
She sets, terribly softly,
Two potted plants on the windowledge
          tic   tic
And bangs shut her window.

A man leaves a doorway tic toc tic toc tic toc tic hurrah toc splat
    on Avenue C tic etc and turns the corner.
Banking the same corner
A pigeon coasts 5th Street in shadows,
Looks for altitude, surmounts the rims of buildings,
And turns white.
The babybirds pipe down. It is day.

   2

In sunlight on the Avenue
The Jew rocks along in a black fur shtraimel,
Black robe, black knickers, black knee-stockings,
Black shoes. His beard like a sod-bottom
Hides the place where he wears no tie.
A dozen children troop after him, barbels flying,
In skullcaps. They are Reuben, Simeon, Levi, Judah, Issachar,
    Zebulun, Benjamin, Dan, Naphtali, Gad, Asher.
With the help of the Lord they will one day become
Courtiers, thugs, rulers, rabbis, asses, adders, wrestlers, bakers,
    poets, cartpushers, infantrymen.

The old man is sad-faced. He is near burial
And one son is missing. The women who bore him sons
And are past bearing mourn for the son
And for the father, wondering if the man will go down
Into the grave of a son mourning, or if at the last
The son will put his hands on the eyes of his father.

The old man wades toward his last hour.
On 5th Street, between Avenues A and B,

In sunshine, in his private cloud, Bunko Certified Embalmer,
Cigar in his mouth, nose to the wind, leans
At the doorway of Bunko's Funeral Home & Parlour,
Glancing west toward the Ukrainians, eastward idly
Where the Jew rocks toward his last hour.

Sons, grandsons at his heel, the old man
Confronts the sun. He does not feel its rays
Through his beard, he does not understand
Fruits and vegetables live by the sun.
Like his children he is sallow-faced, he sees
A blinding signal in the sky, he smiles.

Bury me not Bunko damned Catholic I pray you in Egypt.

3

From the Station House
Under demolishment on Houston
To the Power Station on 14th,
Jews, blacks, Puerto Ricans
Walk in the spring sunlight.

The Downtown Talmud Torah
Blosztein's Cutrate Bakery
Areceba Panataria Hispano
Peanuts Dried Fruit Nuts & Canned Goods
Productos Tropicales
Appetizing Herring Candies Nuts
Nathan Kugler Chicken Store Fresh Killed Daily
Little Rose Restaurant

Rubinstein the Hatter Mens Boys Hats Caps Furnishings
J. Herrmann Dealer in All Kinds of Bottles
Natural Bloom Cigars
Blony Bubblegum
Mueren las Cucarachas Super Potente Garantizada de Matar las
    Cucarachas mas Resistentes
Wenig מצבות
G. Schnee Stairbuilder
Everyouth la Original Loción Eterna Juventud Satisfacción
    Dinero Devuelto
Happy Days Bar & Grill

Through dust-stained windows over storefronts,
Curtains drawn aside, onto the Avenue
Thronged with Puerto Ricans, blacks, Jews,
Baby carriages stuffed with groceries and babies,
The old women peer, blessed damozels
Sitting up there young forever in the cockroached rooms,
Eating fresh-killed chicken, productos tropicales,
Appetizing herring, canned goods, nuts;
They puff out smoke from Natural Bloom Cigars
And one day they puff like Blony Bubblegum.

From a rooftop a boy fishes at the sky,
Around him a flock of pigeons fountains,
Blown down and swirling up again, seeking the sky.
A red kite wriggles like a tadpole
Into the sky beyond them, crosses
The sun, lays bare its own crossed skeleton.
To fly from this place—to roll
On some bubbly blacktop in the summer,

To run under a rain of pigeon plumes, to be
Tarred, and feathered with birdshit, Icarus,

In Kugler's glass headdown dangling by yellow legs.

4

First Sun Day of the year. Tonight,
When the sun will have turned from the earth,
She will appear outside Hy's Luncheonette,
The crone who sells the *News* and the *Mirror*,
The oldest living thing on Avenue C,
Outdating much of its brick and mortar.
If you ask for the *News* she gives you the *Mirror*
And squints long at the nickel in her hand
Despising it, perhaps, for being a nickel,
And stuffs it in her apron pocket
And sucks her lips. Rain or stars, every night
She is there, squatting on the orange crate,
Issuing out only in darkness, like the cucarachas
And dread nightmares in the chambers overhead.
She can't tell one newspaper from another,
She has forgotten how Nain her dead husband looked,
She has forgotten her children's whereabouts,
Or how many there were, or what the *News*
And *Mirror* tell about that we buy them with nickels.
She is sure only of the look of the nickel
And that there is a Lord in the sky overhead.
She dwells in a flesh that is of the Lord
And drifts out, therefore, only in darkness,
Like the streetlamp outside the Luncheonette

Or the lights in the secret chamber
In the firmament, where Yahweh himself dwells.

Like Magdalene in the Battistero of Saint John
On the carved-up continent, in the land of sun,
She lives shadowed, under a feeble bulb
That lights her face, her crab's hands, her small bulk on the crate.

She is Pulchería mother of murderers and madmen,
She is also Alyona whose neck was a chicken leg.

Mother was it the insufferable wind?
She sucks her lips a little further into the mousehole.
She stares among the stars, and among the streetlamps.

The mystery is hers.

5

That violent song of the twilight!
Now, in the silence, will the motherbirds
Be dead, and the infantbirds
That were in the dawn merely transparent
Unfinished things, nothing but bellies,
Will they have been shoved out
And in the course of a morning, casually,
On scrawny wings, have taken up the life?

6

In the pushcart market, on Sunday,
A crate of lemons discharges light like a battery.

Icicle-shaped carrots that through black soil
Wove away lie like flames in the sun.
Onions with their shirts ripped seek sunlight
On green skins. The sun beats
On beets dirty as boulders in cowfields,
On turnips pinched and gibbous
From budging rocks, on embery sweets,
On Idahos, Long Islands, and Maines,
On horseradishes still growing weeds on the flat ends,
On cabbages lying about like sea-green brains
The skulls have been shucked from,
On tomatoes, undented plum-tomatoes, alligator-skinned
Cucumbers, that float pickled
In the wooden tubs of green skim milk—

Sky-flowers, dirt-flowers, underdirt-flowers,
Those that climbed for the sun in their lives
And those that wormed away—equally uprooted,
Maimed, lopped, shucked, and misaimed.

In the market in Damascus a goat
Came to a stall where twelve goatheads
Were lined up for sale. It sniffed them
One by one. Finally thirteen goats started
Smiling in their faintly sardonic way.

A crone buys a pickle from a crone,
It is wrapped in the *Mirror*,
At home she will open the wrapping, stained,
And stare and stare and stare at it.

And the cucumbers, and the melons,
And the leeks, and the onions, and the garlic.

7

Already the Avenue troughs the light of day.
Southward, toward Houston and Pitt,
Where Avenue C begins, the eastern ranges
Of the wiped-out lives—punks, lushes,
Panhandlers, pushers, rumsoaks, all those
Who took it easy when they should have been out failing at
    something—
The pots-and-pans man pushes his cart,
Through the intersection of the light, at 3rd,
Where sunset smashes on the aluminum of it,
On the bottoms, curves, handles, metal panes,
Mirrors: of the bead-curtained cave under the falls
In Freedom, Seekonk Woods leafing the light out,
Halfway to Kingston where a road branched out suddenly,
Between Pamplonne and Les Salins two meeting paths
Over a sea the green of churchsteeple copper.

Of all places on earth inhabited by men
Why is it we find ourselves on this Avenue
Where the dusk gets worse,
And the mirrorman pushing his heaped mirrors
Into the shadows between 3rd and 2nd
Pushes away a mess of old pots and pans?

The ancient black man sits as usual
Outside the Happy Days Bar & Grill. He wears

Dark glasses. Every once in a while, abruptly,
He starts to sing, chanting in a hoarse, nearly breaking
Voice—

And becomes silent
      Stares into the polaroid Wilderness
Gross-Rosen, Maidanek, Flössenberg, Ravensbruck, Stutthof, Riga,
Bergen-Belsen, Mauthausen, Birkenau, Treblinka, Natzweiler,
Dachau, Buchenwald, Auschwitz—
                Villages,
Pasture-bordered hamlets on the far side of the river.

8

The promise was broken too freely
To them and to their fathers, for them to care.
They survive like cedars on a cliff, roots
Hooked in any crevice they can find.
They walk Avenue C in shadows
Neither conciliating its Baalim
Nor whoring after landscapes of the senses,
Tarig bab el Amoud being in the blood
Fumigated by Puerto Rican cooking.

Among women girthed like cedar trees
Other, slenderer ones appear:
One yellow-haired, in August,
Under shooting stars on the lake, who
Believed in promises that broke by themselves—
In a German flower garden in the Bronx
The wedding of a child and a child, one flesh
Divided in the Adirondack spring—
One who found in the desert city of the West
The first happiness, and fled therefore—
And by a southern sea, in the pines, one loved
Until the mist rose blue in the trees
Around the spiderwebs that kept on shining,
Each day of the shortening summer.

And as rubbish burns
And the pushcarts are loaded
With fruits and vegetables and empty crates
And clank away on iron wheels over cobblestones,
And merchants infold their stores
And the carp ride motionlessly sleeplessly
In the dark tank in the fishmarket,
The figures withdraw into chambers overhead—
In the city of the mind, chambers built
Of care and necessity, where, hands lifted to the blinds,
They glimpse in mirrors backed by the blackness of the world
Awkward, cherished rooms containing the familiar selves.

9

Children set fires in ashbarrels,
Cats prowl the fires, scraps of fishes burn.

A child lay in the flames.
It was not the plan. Abraham
Stood in terror at the duplicity.
Isaac whom he loved lay in the flames.
The Lord turned away washing
His hands without soap and water
Like a common housefly.
The children laugh.
Isaac means *he laughs.*
Maybe the last instant,
The dying itself, *is* easier,
Easier anyway than the hike
From Pitt the blind gut
To the East River of Fishes,
Maybe it is as the poet said,
And the soul turns to thee
O vast and well-veiled Death
And the body gratefully nestles close to thee —

I think of Isaac reading Whitman in Chicago,
The week before he died, coming across
Such a passage and muttering, Oi!
What shit! And smiling, but not for you — I mean,

For *thee*, Sane and Sacred Death!

10

It was Gold's junkhouse, the one the clacking
Carts that little men pad after in harnesses
Picking up bedbugged mattresses, springs
The stubbornness has been loved out of,
Chairs felled by fat, lampshades lights have burned through,
Linoleum the geometry has been scuffed from,
Carriages a single woman's work has brought to wreck,
Would come to in the dusk and unload before,
That the whole neighborhood came out to see
Burning in the night, flames opening out like
Eyelashes from the windows, men firing the tears in,
Searchlights smashing against the brick,
The water blooming up the walls
Like pale trees, reaching into the darkness beyond.

Nobody mourned, nobody stood around in pajamas
And a borrowed coat steaming his nose in coffee.
It was only Gold's junkhouse.
                              But this evening
The neighborhood comes out again, everything
That may abide the fire was made to go through the fire
And it was made clean: a few twisted springs,
Charred mattresses (crawling still, naturally),
Perambulator skeletons, bicycles tied in knots—
In a great black pile at the junkhouse door,
Smelling of burnt rubber and hair. Rustwater
Hangs in icicles over the windows and door,
Like frozen piss aimed at trespassers,
Combed by wind, set overnight. Carriages we were babies in,

Springs that used to resist love, that gave in
And were thrown out like whores—the black
Irreducible heap, mausoleum of what we were—
It is cold suddenly, we feel chilled,
Nobody knows for sure what is left of him.

11

The fishmarket closed, the fishes gone into flesh.
The smelts draped on each other, fat with roe,
The marble cod hacked into chunks on the counter,
Butterfishes mouths still open, still trying to eat,
Porgies with receding jaws hinged apart
In a grimace of dejection, as if like cows
They had died under the sledgehammer, perches
In grass-green armor, spotted squeteagues
In the melting ice meek-faced and croaking no more,
Mud-eating mullets buried in crushed ice,
Tilefishes with scales like bits of chickenfat,
Spanish mackerels with buttercups on the flanks,
Pot-bellied pikes, two-tone flounders
After the long contortion of pushing both eyes
To the brown side that they might look up,
Lying brown side down, like a mass laying-on of hands,
Or the oath-taking of an army.

The only things alive are the carp
That drift in the black tank in the rear,
Kept living for the usual reason, that they have not died,
And perhaps because the last meal was garbage and they might
    begin smelling

On dying, before the customer got halfway home.
They nudge each other, to be netted,
The sweet flesh to be lifted thrashing into the air,
To be slugged, and then to keep on living
While they are opened on the counter.

Fishes do not die exactly, it is more
That they go out of themselves, the visible part
Remains the same, there is little pallor,
Only the cataracted eyes that have not shut ever
Must look through the mist that crazed Homer.

These are the vegetables of the deep,
The Sheol-flowers of darkness, swimmers
Of denser darknesses where the sun's rays bend for the last time
And in the sky there burns this shifty jellyfish
That degenerates and flashes and re-forms.

Fishes are nailed to the wood,
The fishmonger stands like Christ, nailing them to the wood,
He scrapes the knife up the grain, the scales fly,
He unnails them, reverses them, nails them again,
Scrapes and the scales fly. He lops off the heads,
Shakes out the guts as if they did not belong in the first place,
And they are flesh for the first time in their lives.

Dear Frau _____:
     Your husband, _____, died in the Camp Hospital on _____.
May I express my sincere sympathy on your bereavement. _____
was admitted to the Hospital on _____ with severe symptoms of
exhaustion, complaining of difficulties in breathing and pains in the

chest. Despite competent medication and devoted medical attention, it proved impossible, unfortunately, to keep the patient alive. The deceased voiced no final requests.

Camp Commandant, _____

On 5th Street Bunko Certified Embalmer Catholic
Leans in his doorway drawing on a Natural Bloom Cigar.
He looks up the street. Even the Puerto Ricans are Jews
And the Chinese Laundry closes on Saturday.

12

Next door, outside the pink-fronted Bodega Hispano—

(A crying: you imagine
Some baby in its crib, wailing
As if it could foresee everything.
The crying subsides: you imagine
A mother or father clasping
The damned creature in their arms.
It breaks out again, this
Time in a hair-raising shriek—so,
The alleycat, in a pleasant guise,
In the darkness outside, in the alley,
Wauling slowly in its blood.

Another, loftier shrieking
Drowns it out. It begins always
On the high note, over a clang of bells:
Hook & Ladder 11 with an explosion of mufflers
Crab-walking out of 5th Street,

Accelerating up the Avenue, siren
Sliding on the rounded distances,
Returning fainter and fainter,
Like a bee looping away from where you lie in the grass.

The searchlights catch him at the topfloor window,
Trying to move, nailed in place by the shine.

The bells of Saint Brigid's
On Tompkins Square
Toll for someone who has died—
J'oïs la cloche de Serbonne,
Qui toujours à neuf heures sonne
Le Salut que l'Ange prédit…

Expecting the visitation
You lie back on your bed,
The sounds outside
Must be outside. Here
Are only the dead spirituals
Turning back into prayers—
You rise on an elbow
To make sure they come from outside,
You hear nothing, you lay down
Your head on a pillow
Like a pick-up arm—
        swing low
                swing low
                        sweet
        lowsweet—)
—Carols of the Caribbean, plinkings of guitars.

13

The garbage-disposal truck
Like a huge hunched animal
That sucks in garbage in the place
Where other animals evacuate it
Whines, as the cylinder in the rear
Threshes up the trash and garbage,
Where two men in rubber suits
(It must be raining outside)
Heap it in. The groaning motor
Rises to a whine as it grinds in
The garbage, and between-times
Groans. It whines and groans again.
All about it as it moves down
5th Street is the clatter of trashcans,
The crashes of them as the sanitary engineers
Bounce them on the sidewalk.

If it is raining outside
You can only tell by looking
In puddles, under the lifted streetlamps.

It would be the spring rain.

14

Behind the Power Station on 14th, the held breath
Of light, as God is a held breath, withheld,
Spreads the East River, into which fishes leak:
The brown sink or dissolve,

The white float out in shoals and armadas,
Even the gulls pass them up, pale
Bloated socks of riverwater and rotted seed
That swirl on the tide, punched back
To the Hell Gate narrows, and on the ebb
Steam seaward, seeding the sea.

On the Avenue, through air tinted crimson
By neon over the bars, the rain is falling.
You stood once on Houston, among panhandlers and winos
Who weave the eastern ranges, learning to be free,
To not care, to be knocked flat and to get up clear-headed
Spitting the curses out. "Now be nice,"
The proprietor threatens; "Be nice," he cajoles.
"Fuck you," the bum shouts as he is hoisted again,
"God fuck your mother." (In the empty doorway,
Hunched on the empty crate, the crone gives no sign.)

That night a wildcat cab whined crosstown on 7th.
You knew even the traffic lights were made by God,
The red splashes growing dimmer the farther away
You looked, and away up at 14th, a few green stars;
And without sequence, and nearly all at once,
The red lights blinked into green,
And just before there was one complete Avenue of green,
The little green stars in the distance blinked.

It is night, and raining. You look down
Toward Houston in the rain, the living streets,
Where instants of transcendence

Drift in oceans of loathing and fear, like lanternfishes,
Or phosphorous flashings in the sea, or the feverish light
Skin is said to give off when the swimmer drowns at night.

From the blind gut Pitt to the East River of Fishes
The Avenue cobbles a swath through the discolored air,
A roadway of refuse from the teeming shores and ghettos
And the Caribbean Paradise, into the new ghetto and new
        paradise,
This God-forsaken Avenue bearing the initial of Christ
Through the haste and carelessness of the ages,
The sea standing in heaps, which keeps on collapsing,
Where the drowned suffer a C-change,
And remain the common poor.

Since Providence, for the realization of some unknown purpose,
has seen fit to leave this dangerous people on the face of the earth
and did not destroy it...

Listen! the swish of the blood,
The sirens down the bloodpaths of the night,
Bone tapping on the bone, nerve-nets
Singing under the breath of sleep—

We scattered over the lonely seaways,
Over the lonely deserts did we run,
In dark lanes and alleys we did hide ourselves...

The heart beats without windows in its night,
The lungs put out the light of the world as they

Heave and collapse, the brain turns and rattles
In its own black axlegrease—

                        In the nighttime
Of the blood they are laughing and saying,
Our little lane, what a kingdom it was!
                               oi weih, oi weih

Flower Herding
on Mount Monadnock

PART I

The River That Is East

1

Buoys begin clanging like churches
And peter out. Sunk to the gunwhales
In their shapes, tugs push upstream.
A carfloat booms down, sweeping past
Illusory suns that blaze in puddles
On the shores where it rained, past the Navy Yard,
Under the Williamsburg Bridge
That hangs facedown from its strings
Over which the Jamaica Local crawls,
Through white-winged gulls which shriek
And flap from the water and sideslip in
Over a chaos of illusions, dangling
Limp red hands, and screaming as they touch.

2

A boy swings his legs from the pier,
His days go by. Tugs and carfloats go by,
Each prow pushing a whitecap. On his deathbed
Kane remembered the abrupt, missed Grail
Called Rosebud, Gatsby may have flashed back
To his days digging clams in Little Girl Bay
In Minnesota, Nick fished in dreamy Michigan,
Gant had his memories, Griffiths, those
Who went baying after the immaterial
And whiffed its strange dazzle in a blonde

In a canary convertible, who died
Thinking of the Huck Finns of themselves
On the old afternoons, themselves like this boy
Swinging his legs, who sees the *Ile de France*
Come in, and wonders if in some stateroom
There is not a sick-hearted heiress sitting
Drink in hand, saying to herself his name.

3

A man stands on the pier.
He has long since stopped wishing his heart were full
Or his life dear to him.
He watches the snowfall hitting the dirty water.
He thinks: Beautiful. Beautiful.
If I were a gull I would be one with white wings,
I would fly out over the water, explode, and
Be beautiful snow hitting the dirty water.

4

And thou, River of Tomorrow, flowing...
We stand on the shore, which is mist beneath us,
And regard the onflowing river. Sometimes
It seems the river stops and the shore
Flows into the past. What is this river
But the one that drags the things we love,
Processions of debris like floating lamps
Toward the radiance in which they go out?
No, it is the River that is East, known once
From a high window in Brooklyn, in agony—river

On which a door locked to the water floats,
A window sash paned with brown water, a whiskey crate,
Barrel staves, sun spokes, feathers of the birds,
A breadcrust, a rat, spittle, butts, and peels,
The immaculate stream, heavy, and swinging home again.

The Homecoming of Emma Lazarus

1

Having no father anymore, having got up
In England without hope, having sailed the strewn
Atlantic and been driven under Bedloe
In the night, where the Green Lady lifts
Over that slow, bleating, tragic harbor

Her burning hand, Emma came floating home,
To the thick, empty whistling of the tugs.
Thoreau's pocket compass had been her keepsake,
She made her way in without it, through the fog.
It was hard for her, coming in to die,

A little unfair, her father having died already.
In the attic on Union Square? Thrown out? Ah,
Somewhere in the mess of things! From Governor's Island
A bugler's loneliest notes roll slowly in
And birds rock in the fog on the slapping waves.

2

As a child she had chased a butterfly
Through Battery Park, possibly the only one
In Manhattan that afternoon, its wind-thin
Wings making cathedral windows in the sun,

While the despised grandmother
With the gleety leashes, cruddy with age,
Of her eyebeams, held on. Her doughy
Ears, too, must have been golden in the sun.

It was toward you, gilded in the day's going down,
Green Lady, that we crawled—but from what ground of nausea
Had we turned, what relinquished plot of earth
Had we reviled, which was, anyway, the earth?

3

Dark-haired, ephebic Emma, she knew
The night she floated into New York Harbor
That Atlantis had sunk while she was abroad,
She could see its rainbows shining queerly
The many thousand leagues of her life away—

Weekends on Union Square, from her father's shaving mug
She blew bubbles crawling with colors that buoyed
Into the sunshine, she made up rhymes,
She skipped rope, she sat on his knee as he put
Lilacs in her hair. Everybody loved her!

And on the last ride across 14th,
Did the English success suddenly become nothing,
Did the American childhood, including its lasting affliction,
A longing to be English, turn out to be
The paradise she died longing for?

4

Facing the Old World the Green Lady whispers, "Eden!"
Seeing her looking so trim in her American verdigris
They thought she was saying how it was here.
Seeing her gazing out to sea we read it as pure nostalgia.
Vacuumed in the wind from the Dry Cleaning Store
She may, herself, have wondered which she meant.

She crouches on the floor. She read once,
In the paper, a poem she had composed herself.
Was it just poetry, all that? It was pretty,
There is nothing she can do about it, it really was.
Her arm lies along the bench, her hand
Hangs over the edge as if she has just let something drop.

She has wept a long time now, and now poetry
Can do no more to her. Her shoulder shrugs as though
To drive away birds which probably weren't intending
To alight. In the Harbor the conscript bugler
Blows the old vow of acceptance into the night—
It fades, and the wounds of all we had accepted open.

Old Arrivals

Molded in verdigris
Shortly before she died
The Lady stands by herself,
Her electrical hand on fire.

They too in the Harbor
That chops the light to pieces
Looked up at her hand, burning,
Hair, flesh, blood, bone.

They floated in at night
On black water, cargoes
Which may not go back, waves
Breaking the rocks they break on.

Calcutta Visits

Overhead the fan wobbles on its axle.
In Delhi, on Gandhi's tomb, it said *Hai Ram* ("an old cry").
On Sudden Street they call, "Hey Johnny,
Nice girl? Chinese, Indian, European, Mixed?"
She taps a foot, finicks with phonograph needles,
Fools with buttons. "No like dance,"
She announces, collapsing on the carpet.
The bird will leave this branch at dawn
And fly away. For one full day remember her.

From this blue window? this blue, zigzagging street?
"*Five? Five* already? Ah, den, come morning…"
A man in white skids toward your knees,
"A morsel! A morsel!" The only city
In the world where the beggars have read Dickens,
Says the Oxford Indian of his first homecoming,
As he sits up there in the Grand Hotel,
Among bribed, sleepy bellhops, drinking himself blind,
While the fan prowls the ceiling as in a zoo.

Floodtime. Cabs practically floating through town.
The driver sizes me up in the rearview mirror
With black, mystical eyes: how exactly
To soak me … A Bengal poet, disciple of Tagore,
His tongue flickering through his talk like a serpent's,
Looks from his window on the city. He says
Each day he has to transcend its pain anew.
His face darkens in the light from the window.
It is his pain, by the love that asks no way out.

Doppelgänger

1

I have to bribe the policeman
To keep him from arresting the driver
For trying to make me overpay him, which I've just done.

A sailor staggers up,
All his money blown on thieves he cries,
I pay him and he goes off hunting more thieves.

The fan whips up the heat,
The ice turns to slush
Before you can throw it into your whiskey.

2

I remember at daybreak,
The air on the point of cooling
Was just starting to heat up,

I heard a voice in the distance,
I looked up, far away,
There at the beginning of the world

I could make out a beggar,
Down the long street he was calling *Galway!*
I started toward him and began calling *Galway!*

To a Child in Calcutta

Dark child in my arms, eyes
The whites of them just like mine
Gazing with black, shined canniness
At mine like blue-green agates,

Whom I held as a passerby
A few stricken days down Bandook Gulli,
While they were singing, upstairs,
Everyone in Calcutta is knocking at my door,

You are my conqueror! and you were
Calmly taking in my colored eyes and
Skin burned and thin and
Browned hardly at all by your Bengal sun:

If they show you, when you reach my age,
The blown-up snapshot they took of the stranger
Holding all you once were in his arms,
What will you be able to think, then,

Of the one who came from some elsewhere
And took you in his arms
And let you know the touch of a stranger
And the old warmth in a paw from nowhere,

But that in his nowhere
He will be dying, letting go his hold
On all for which his heart tore itself
As when they snapped you in his arms like his child,

And going by the photograph
That there was this man, his hair in his eyes,
His hand bigger than your whole head,
Who held you when helplessly

You let him, that between him and you
Were this gesture and this allowance
And he is your stranger father
And he dies in a strange land, which is his own.

In Calcutta, I thought,
Every pimp, taxidriver, whore, and beggar,
Dowsed for me through the alleys day and night—
In Bandook Gulli I came upon you,

On a street crossed by fading songs
I held you in my arms
Until you slept, in these arms,
In rags, in the pain of a little flesh.

Kyoto Prints

1

In the green air
Of before the dawn
The gutturals of the prayer
Pile up in formal hiccups.

2

The lake
Every point on whose shore
Remains out of sight of some other point
Is drawn from the kokorai,
A character drawn from the heart.
In it is a flaw called the Pure Land.

3

Miko pick their way past
A phallic, thousand-year
Old gravestone
With chalk faces, on big shoes,
Pucka pucka pucka pucka

4

After the Ceremony of Kō
The girl draws out the coals
And pokes nine vents in the clay
To let out the fire smell.

5

Tied to a few leaves
Attached loosely to the air
In the garden of moss and pine
An old eye with a spider in it
No longer troubles to look out,
A common disease of the eye.
(It has a pretty name:
I-Saw-the-Ghost-of-a-Flower.)

Koisimi Buddhist of Altitudes

He sees a skinny waterfall hanging
Like a bare root, a shape seeking water
Down which the particles of water crawl,
And climbs, crawling up the shined
Rock rubbing his fingerprints off,
And looks from the top at the land, as it was,
Clawed from within, perfectly unbroken.
In the glare, he waits, he hears
On the horizon the whine of wind
Machining its way to where he is.
The eddies begin picking up speed,
Sunlight and rock are circling
Around him, lose hold, skid
Some degrees, appear to recover,
And now skid all the way out, and vanish.
What is this wind? Koisimi challenges.
It is not I, he knows, and leans
In any direction, which is the way.

Room of Return

Room over the Hudson
Where a naked light bulb
Lights coat hangers, whiskey bottles,
Umbrellas, anti-war tracts, poems,
A potted plant trimmed to a crucifixion,

From which, out the front window,
It is possible to watch
The *Vulcania* or the *France*
Or a fat *Queen*
Steaming through the buildings across the street,

To which every night
The alleycat sneaks up
To slop his saucer
Of fresh cream on the fire escape,
Washing down his rat,

Room crossed by wind from
Air conditioners' back ends,
By the clicking at all hours of invisible looms,
By cries of the night-market, hoofbeats, horns,
By bleats of lost boats on the Hudson,

Room
Where I switch the light on,
Tiny glimmer again in this city
Among all the others after an absence of years.

For Denise Levertov

Denise when you recited
With your intense unmusical voice
Poems on the objects of faith,
Buildings, rocks, birds, oranges,
A bum stood outside on Bleecker
Looking in through the glass
At you sitting in your green robe
Facing the Old World longhand
Repository of your utter, gently uttered
Solitude. Had you glanced up,
Had you seen his liquored eye,
The mowed cornfield of his gawk,
Maybe you would have paused
And seen him eye to eye,
And then gone on, in a room
Of cigarette smoke and coffee smells
And faithful friends, the hapless
Witness crying again in your breast.

Under the Williamsburg Bridge

I broke bread
At the riverbank,
I saw the black gull
Fly back black and crossed
By the decaying Paragon sign in Queens
Over ripped water, it screamed
Killing the ceremony of the dove,
Its wing muscles
Pulling apart my bones.

Tomorrow,
On the bridge,
In some riveted cranny in the sky,
The great and wondrous sun will be shining
On a spider wrapping its fly in spittle-strings.

For Robert Frost

1

Why do you talk so much
Robert Frost? One day
I drove up to Ripton to ask,

I stayed the whole day
And never got the chance
To put the question.

I drove off at dusk
Worn out and aching
In both ears. Robert Frost,

Were you shy as a boy?
Do you go on making up
For some long period of solitude?

Is it that talk
Doesn't have to be metered and rhymed?
Is talk distracting from something worse?

2

I saw you once on the TV,
Unsteady at the lectern,
The flimsy white leaf
Of hair standing straight up

In the wind, among top hats,
Old farmer and son
Of worse winters than this,
Stopped in the first dazzle

Of the District of Columbia,
Suddenly having to pay
For the cheap onionskin,
The worn-out ribbon, the eyes
Wrecked from writing poems
For us—stopped,
Lonely before millions,
The paper jumping in your grip,

And as the Presidents
Also on the platform
Began flashing nervously
Their Presidential smiles
For the harmless old guy,
And poets watching on the TV
Started thinking, Well that's
The end of *that* tradition,

And the managers of the event
Said, Boys this is it,
This sonofabitch poet
Is gonna croak,
Putting the paper aside
You drew forth
From your great faithful heart
The poem.

3

Once, walking in winter in Vermont,
In the snow, I followed a set of footprints
That aimed for the woods. At the verge
I could make out, "far in the pillared dark,"
An old creature in a huge, clumsy overcoat,
Lifting his great boots through the drifts,
Going as if to die among "those dark trees"
Of his own country. I watched him go,

Past a house, quiet, warm and light,
A farm, a countryside, a woodpile in its slow
Smokeless burning, alder swamps ghastly white,
Tumultuous snows, blanker whitenesses,
Into the pathless wood, one eye weeping,
The dark trees, for which no saying is dark enough,
Which mask the gloom and lead on into it,
The bare, the withered, the deserted.

There were no more cottages.
Soft bombs of dust falling from the boughs,
The sun shining no warmer than the moon,
He had outwalked the farthest city light,
And there, clinging to the perfect trees,
A last leaf. What was it?
What was that whiteness?—white, uncertain—
The night too dark to know.

4

He turned. *Love,*
Love of things, duty, he said,
And made his way back to the shelter
No longer sheltering him, the house
Where everything turned into words,

Where he would think on the white wave,
Folded back, that rides in place on the obscure
Pouring of this life to the sea—
And seal the loose lips
Of the darkness with the *mot juste.*

5

Poet of the country of white houses,
Of clearings going out to the dark wall of woods
Frayed along the skyline, you who nearly foreknew
The next lines of poems you suddenly left off writing,
Who dwelt in access to that which other men
Have burned all their lives to get near, who heard
The high wind, in gusts, seething
From far off, coming through the trees exactly
To this place where it must happen, who spent
Your life on the point of giving yourself away
To the dark trees, the dissolving woods,
Into which you go at last, heart in hand, deep in:

When we think of a man who was cursed
Neither with the all-lovingness of Walt Whitman

Nor with Melville's anguish to know and to suffer,
And yet cursed … A man, what shall I say,
Vain, not fully convinced he was dying, whose calling
Was to set up in the wilderness of his country,
At whatever cost, a man who would be his own man,
We think of you. And from the same doorway
At which you lived, between the house and the woods,
We see your old footprints going away across
The great Republic, Frost, up memorized slopes,
Down hills floating by heart on the bulldozed land.

PART II

Tillamook Journal

I have come here
From Chicago, packing
A sleeping bag, a pan
To melt snow for drinking,
Dried apricots, tea,
A great boiled beef-heart.

Two loggers drove me
As far in as they could get,
Two gunnysack loggers of the Burn,
Owning a truck and a dozer, a few cables
And saws, who drag out
The sound heartwood for money.

They said there'd
Been a prospector here a year ago,
Hunting uranium or gold,
They would run across him,
A little, swaying heap of gear,
With a Geiger counter

Lashed on like an extra heart,
They said they would find him
Mumbling about metal while
Thrashing up some avalanching gravel.
Around January he was ready
To settle for anything at all.
When spring came he vanished.

I set out walking,
Up to my ankles in gravel,
Grappling at roots and rocks.
At last I was climbing up
On my hands and knees
As though I'd come here begging.

From the top of Cedar Butte
The whole compass is visible,
To the west the Pacific
Lying out flat and shiny,
North and east, hill
After hill of white snags.

To the south, white stumps, white logs,
Washing to the valleys, bleeding scarps,
Lopped spurs, empty streambeds.
The land, split and cracked
Under the crisscross of logging roads,
Oozing down its ravines.

It is twenty-five years
Since the first blue-white puff was sighted.
Convicts have planted saplings
By the coast, schoolboys
Have planted by the highway,
So far little catches.

To the north, on the hills
Loggers can't reach,
Great virgin stands of snags
Burnt clean and bleached
In the distance keeping on
Blurring to look like smoke.

Big, immaculate snowflakes
Have been coming down, melting
On touching. All night,
As I lay trying for sleep,
I listened to Kilchis
River grinding its rocks and boulders.

The ravine is a mass of slash slippery
With rain and snow. Tree
Trunks cross and lock each other
Blocking the water,
Intricately grained
Rims for the little waterfalls.

A mule deer joined me,
Leading like a scout,
When I turned off and climbed
He stopped too, and sadly—I found myself
Sadly thinking—watched my going.
Birds wrangled and chirped.

I was sitting under
The last knoll,
Gnawing the last of the heart,
Looking back at the Burn
As it went out in the twilight,
Its crags broken, its valleys

Soaked in night, another
Plundered breast of the world.
I scrambled to my feet
And climbed, I could hear my heart
Beating in the air around me,
And came over the last summit

Into a dark wind blasting
Out of the blackness.
Behind me snow was still falling.
Before me the Pacific
Fell with long triple crashes on the shore.
It was only steps to the unburnable sea.

On Hardscrabble Mountain

1

On old slashed spruce boughs
Buoying me up off the snow
I stretched out on the slope,
Now and then a bit of snow
Would slide quietly from a branch,

Once a deerfly came by,

I could see off for about a hundred miles.

2

I waked with a start,
The sun had crawled off me,
I was shivering in thick blue shadows,
Sap was sticking me to the spruce boughs,

The wind was starting to rise.

3

On the way down, passing
A little graveyard in the woods,
I gave a thought to the human bones buried there,

I breathed something like a prayer
To a bear just shutting his eyes,
To a skunk dozing off,
To a marmot with yellow belly,
To a dog-faced hedgehog,
To a dormouse with a paunch and ears like leaves or wings.

On Frozen Fields

We walk across the snow.
A moon can be eating itself out,
Meteors can be flaring to death on earth,
The aurora borealis can be blooming and seething.
We walk arm in arm, and we are happy.

In Fields of Summer

The sun rises,
The goldenrod blooms,
My own life is adrift in me,
In my heart and hands, in my teeth,
It shines up at the old heron
Who holds out his drainpipe of a neck
And creaks along in the blue.

The goldenrod shines with its life, too,
And the great field wavers and flakes,
The rumble of the bees deepens,
A phoebe flutters up,
A lark bursts up all dew.

A Bird Comes Back

Only the head and the shoulders, only
The bust of a bird really,
Cochineal and emerald, appears,
Stinging the blossoms, there
At the open window, in the phlox,
Where there are, already,
Bees and a few white butterflies.
The timbers of the house
Shift sidewise, like stove grates,
One of the too-frequent settlings.
I think of Emily Dickinson's hummingbird.
Odd to see him now
With nothing in back of him
But New Hampshire fifty miles away and badly faded.

Cells Breathe in the Emptiness

The flowers turn to husks
And the great trees seem suddenly to die
And rocks and old weasel bones lose
The little life they had:
The air becomes so still
It gives the ears something like the bends.
Listen! That would be the sound of the teeth
Of a sloppy green cabbageworm
Eating its route through a turnip
Inside the compost heap
Now snarling like a petite chainsaw, now droning.
A butterfly battens on a buttercup,
From the junkpile jukes up a junco.

Poem of Night

1

I move my hand over
Slopes, falls, lumps of sight,
Lashes barely able to be touched,
Lips that give way so easily
It's a shock to feel under them
The hard smile of bones.

Muffled a little, barely cloaked,
Zygoma, maxillary, turbinate.

2

I put my hand
On the side of your face,
You lean your head a little
Into my hand—and so,
I know you're a dormouse
Taken up in winter sleep,
A lonely, stunned weight.

3

A cheekbone,
A curved piece of brow,
A pale eyelid
Float in the dark,

And now I make out
An eye, dark,
Wormed with far-off, unaccountable lights.

4

Hardly touching, I hold
What I can only think of
As some deepest of memories in my arms,
Not mine, but as if the life in me
Were slowly remembering what it is.

You lie here now in your physicalness,
This beautiful degree of reality.

5

Now the day, raft that breaks up, comes on.

I think of a few bones
Floating on a river at night,
The starlight blowing in place on the water,
The river leaning like a wave toward the emptiness.

Nightfall of the Real

Swallows dart at one another
Across the curve of the moon. Two
Ravens tumble at the cliff and fall away. On the port
The orange, white, and blue umbrellas
Which have been turning all day to the sun
Fold themselves. In the Bar des Guitares
They are raking the strings.
Mullets are leaping in the straits.

   ✑

On a table set by heart
In the last sun of the day
Olives, three fishes,
Bread, a bottle of rosé.

A rainbow crosses a fish,
A glass blossoms and reblossoms,
Flesh slides off bones which were,
We now see, only stabbing it.

Darkness sticks itself
To empty spines. Night climbs
In glasses. A breeze. Low voices.
Paths floating on earth.

   ✑

Olives, bread,
Fishes, pink wine:
Gradually in the dusk
A crackling across stones.

To this table one came,
Came and ate, tore actual bread,
Felt physical drink touch his soul,
Here conversed, here laughed.

*

Four faces look in
On a vanished room—the vineyard,
The olive grove, the stones,
The green sea—and themselves begin vanishing.

Out in the dark
A distant dull splash of a fish.
Yet again. Sick of weight
It leans up through its eerie life
Toward the night-flash of its emblemhood.

*

Spoon, table, mirrors,
Green portrait of vase of flowers,
Vase of flowers,
Each streaked fatally with dusk.

The light grows dim,
The richest time, which is twilight.
On the shore lies
A fern fishy and glittering.

Middle of the Way

1

I wake in the night,
An ache in the shoulder blades.
I lie amazed under the trees
That creak a little in the dark,
The giant trees of the world.

I lie on earth the way
Flames lie in the woodpile,
Or as an imprint, in sperm or egg, of what is to be.
I love the earth, and always
In its darknesses I am a stranger.

2

6 A.M. Water frozen again. Melted it and made tea. Ate a raw egg and the last orange. Refreshed by a long sleep. The trail practically indistinguishable under 8" of snow. 9:30 A.M. Snow up to my knees in places. Sweat begins freezing under my shirt when I stop to rest. The woods are filled, anyway, with the windy noise of the first streams. 10:30 A.M. The sun at last. The snow starts to melt off the boughs at once, falling with little ticking sounds. Mist clouds are lying in the valleys. 11:45 A.M. Slow, glittering breakers roll in on the beaches ten miles away, very blue and calm. 12 noon. An inexplicable sense of joy, as if some happy news had been transmitted to me directly, bypassing the brain. 2 P.M. From the top of Gauldy I looked back into Hebo valley. Castle Rock sticks into a cloud. A cool breeze comes up from the valley, it is a fresh, earthly

wind and tastes of snow and trees. It is not like those transcendental breezes that make the heart ache. It brings happiness. 2:30 P.M. Lost the trail. A woodpecker watches me wade about through the snow trying to locate it. The sun has gone back of the trees. 3:10 P.M. Still hunting for the trail. It is getting cold. From an elevation I have an open view to the SE, a world of timberless, white hills, rolling, weirdly wrinkled. Above them a pale half moon. 3:45 P.M. Going on by map and compass. A minute ago a deer fled touching down every fifteen feet or so. 7:30 P.M. Made camp near the head of Alder Creek. Trampled a bed into the snow and filled it with boughs. Concocted a little fire in the darkness. Ate pork and beans. A slug or two of whiskey burnt my throat. The night very clear. Very cold. That half moon is up there and a lot of stars have come out among the treetops. The fire has fallen to coals.

3

The coals go out,
The last smoke wavers up
Losing itself in the stars.
This is my first night to lie
In the uncreating dark.

In the human heart
There sleeps a green worm
That has spun the heart about itself,
And that shall dream itself black wings
One day to break free into the black sky.

I leave my eyes open
And lie here and forget our life.
All I see is that we float out
Into the emptiness, among the great stars,
On this little vessel without lights.

I know that I love the day,
The sun on the mountain, the Pacific
Shiny and accomplishing itself in breakers,
But I know I live half alive in the world,
Half my life belongs to the wild darkness.

Ruins Under the Stars

1

All day under acrobat
Swallows I have sat, beside ruins
Of a plank house sunk up to its windows
In burdock and raspberry cane,
The roof dropped, the foundation broken in,
Nothing left perfect but the axe-marks on the beams.

2

Overhead the skull-hill rises
Crossed on top by the stunted apple,
Infinitely beyond it, older than love or guilt,
The stars lie ready to jump and sprinkle out of space.

Every night under those thousand lights
An owl dies, a snake sloughs its skin,
A man in a dark pasture
Feels a homesickness he does not understand.

3

Sometimes I see them,
The south-going Canada geese,
At evening, coming down
In pink light, over the pond, in great,
Loose, always-dissolving V's—
I go out into the field to hear
The cold, lonely yelping
Of their tranced bodies in the sky.

4

This morning I watched
Milton Norway's sky-blue Ford
Dragging its ass down the dirt road
On the other side of the valley.

Later, off in the woods,
A chainsaw was agonizing across the top of some stump.
A while ago the tracks of a little, snowy,
SAC bomber crawled across heaven.

What of that hairstreak
That was flopping and batting about
Deep in the goldenrod—
Did she not know, either, where she was going?

5

The bats come spelling the swallows.
In the smoking heap of old antiques
The porcupine-crackle starts up again,
The bone-saw, the ur-music of our sphere.
Up there the stars rustling and whispering.

Tree from Andalusia

This bleached tree
Dumped on the Sagaponack beach...

The wind has lifted and now seethes
Far up among the invisible stars.

Once on Ferry Street, at night,
Among TO LET signs and closed wholesalers.

From some loft a phrase of jazz,
y recuerdo una brisa triste por los olivos.

The wind starts fluting
In our teeth, in our ears.

It whines down the harmonica
Of the fingerbones, moans at the skull.

Blown on by their death
The things of earth whistle and cry out.

Spindrift

1

Sitting on this tree thrown up
From the sea, its tangle of roots
Letting the wind go through,
I look down the beach: at old
Horseshoe crabs, broken skates,
Sand dollars, sea horses, as though
Only primeval creatures get destroyed,
At chunks of sea-mud still quivering,
At the light glinting off the water
And the billion facets of the sand,
At their moment of shining the wind
Blows over dunes as they creep.

2

Sit down
By the clanking shore
Of this bitter, beloved sea,

Pluck
Shells from the icy surf,
Fans of gold light, sunbursts,

Lift one to the sun
As a sign you accept to go
When the time comes to the shrine of the dead.

3

This bleached root
Drifted from some other shore,
Brittle, cold, practically weightless, worn
Down to the lost grip it always essentially was.

If it has lost hold
It at least keeps
The shape of what it held,
And is the hand itself
Of that gravel, one of earth's
Wandering icons of "to have."

4

I sit listening
To the surf as it falls,
The power and inexhaustible freshness of the sea,
The suck and inner boom
As a wave tears free and crashes back
In overlapping thunders going away down the beach.

It is the most we know of time,
And it is our undermusic of eternity.

5

I think of how I
Sat by a dying woman,
Her shell of a hand

Wet and cold in both of mine,
Light, nearly out, existing as smoke.

I remember the glow of her wan, absorbed smile.

6

Under the wind
That moans in the grass
And whistles through crabs' claws
I sit holding this little lamp,
This icy fan of the sun.

Across gull tracks
And wind ripples in the sand
The wind seethes. Footprints behind me
Slogging for the absolute
Already begin vanishing.

7

What does he really love,
That old man,
His wrinkled eyes
Tortured by smoke,
Walking in the ungodly
Rasp and cackle of old flesh?

The swan dips its head
And peers at the mystic
In-life of the sea,
The gull drifts up
And eddies toward heaven,
The breeze in its arms...

Nobody likes to die
But an old man
Can know
A gratefulness
Toward time that kills him,
Everything he loved was made of it.

Flower Herding on Mount Monadnock

1

I can support it no longer.
Laughing ruefully at myself
For all I claim to have suffered
I get up. Damned nightmarer!

It is New Hampshire out here,
It is nearly the dawn.
The song of the whippoorwill stops
And the dimension of depth seizes everything.

2

The whistlings of a peabody bird go overhead
Like a needle pushed five times through the air,
They enter the leaves, and come out little changed.

The air is so still
That as they go off through the trees
The love songs of birds do not get any fainter.

3

The last memory I have
Is of a flower that cannot be touched,

Through the bloom of which, all day,
Fly crazed, missing bees.

4

As I climb sweat gets up my nostrils,
For an instant I think I am at the sea,

One summer off Cap Ferrat we watched a black seagull
Straining for the dawn, we stood in the surf,

Grasshoppers splash up where I step,
The mountain laurel crashes at my thighs.

5

There is something joyous in the elegies
Of birds. They seem
Caught up in a formal delight,
Though the mourning dove whistles of despair.

But at last in the thousand elegies
The dead rise in our hearts,
On the brink of our happiness we stop
Like someone on a drunk starting to weep.

6

I kneel at a pool,
I look through my face
At the bacteria I think
I see crawling through the moss.

My face sees me,
The water stirs, the face,
Looking preoccupied,
Gets knocked from its bones.

7

I weighed eleven pounds
At birth, having stayed on
Two extra weeks in the womb.
Tempted by room and fresh air
I came out big as a policeman,
Blue-faced, with narrow red eyes.
It was eight days before the doctor
Would scare my mother with me.

Turning and craning in the vines
I can make out through the leaves
The old, shimmering nothingness, the sky.

8

Green, scaly moosewoods ascend,
Tenants of the shaken paradise,

At every wind last night's rain
Comes splattering from the leaves,

It drops in flurries and lies there,
The footsteps of some running start.

9

From a rock
A waterfall,
A single trickle like a strand of wire,
Breaks into beads halfway down.

I know
The birds fly off
But the hug of the earth wraps
With moss their graves and the giant boulders.

10

In the forest I discover a flower.

The invisible life of the thing
Goes up in flames that are invisible,
Like cellophane burning in the sunlight.

It burns up. Its drift is to be nothing.

In its covertness it has a way
Of uttering itself in place of itself,
Its blossoms claim to float in the Empyrean,

A wrathful presence on the blur of the ground.

The appeal to heaven breaks off.
The petals begin to fall, in self-forgiveness.
It is a flower. On this mountainside it is dying.

GALWAY KINNELL is a former MacArthur fellow and has been the state poet of Vermont. In 1982 his *Selected Poems* won the Pulitzer Prize and the National Book Award. He has translated works of Bonnefoy, Lorca, Rilke, and Villon. Kinnell is Erich Maria Remarque Professor of Creative Writing at New York University. He lives in New York City and Vermont.